POSITION PRIMER

FOR THE GUITAR STUDENT

Ralph Louis Scicchitano

"COMMAND OF MOVABLE SCALE FORMS IS PERTINENT TO MASTERING THE FINGERBOARD AND KEYS."

POSITION PRIMER FOR THE GUITAR STUDENT
COMMAND OF MOVABLE SCALE FORMS IS PERTINENT TO
MASTERING THE FINGERBOARD AND KEYS.

Author Credits: Anytime Publications

iUniverse books may be ordered through booksellers or by contacting:

iUniverse
1663 Liberty Drive
Bloomington, IN 47403
www.iuniverse.com
1-800-Authors (1-800-288-4677)

Because of the dynamic nature of the Internet, any web addresses or links contained in this book may have changed since publication and may no longer be valid. The views expressed in this work are solely those of the author and do not necessarily reflect the views of the publisher, and the publisher hereby disclaims any responsibility for them.

Any people depicted in stock imagery provided by Getty Images are models,
and such images are being used for illustrative purposes only.
Certain stock imagery © Getty Images.

ISBN: 978-1-5320-9926-7 (sc)
ISBN: 978-1-5320-9927-4 (e)

Library of Congress Control Number: 2020906900

Print information available on the last page.

iUniverse rev. date: 04/29/2020

Table of Contents

PREFACE

This method was composed to fill a need for a specialized guitar study for guitar students of all ages. <u>Position Primer for the Guitar Student</u> is an organized, systematic, simple, fun, and informative approach to learning the fingerboard, movable scale forms, keys, improvisation, and technique. This is accomplished by concentrating on the various areas or positions of the fingerboard. You will find these studies to be a practical, refreshing alternative to traditional scale studies.

Before starting, you should have a solid command of 1st position in areas of reading, memorization and technique. This includes knowing the names of the notes and being able to recognize the notation for open strings, naturals, sharps and flats on the first four frets without hesitation. All four fingers of the left hand should be equally developed in the areas of coordination and dexterity. Many students tend to "favor" the naturally stronger index and middle fingers. However, it is important for all four to be developed equally.

Position is generally considered to be a four adjacent fret segment of the fingerboard. Position number is determined by the fret where the first finger naturally falls. The first and fourth finger may sometimes stretch out of position. However, the four adjacent fret concept is a good general format and is easy to apply to movable scale forms.

Often, students ask: "If I can play a note in one place, why bother to learn the same note somewhere else?" Actually, when given the chance to learn more of the fingerboard, you will probably prefer to play in positions other than first. Open strings are difficult to control. Convenience, fingering logic, phrasing, key, sound range, and personal preference dictate where on the fingerboard to play.

Holding the Guitar, Posture and Finger Placement

You will achieve best results if the instrument is held correctly and if you are sitting properly. Elevate the leg supporting the guitar with a foot rest. One of the best sitting positions is the "classical" method, with the legs apart and the guitar resting on the left leg, elevated with a foot rest. This should slant the guitar neck "uphill". Keep your back straight, left thumb low, pointing up, slightly to the left and wrist out. Play on your fingertips, close to the fret bars. Keep the first joints of your fingers curved. Relax and avoid tension.

How to Study this Method

This will be easy to understand. On each lesson there will be a warmup scale to memorize. To master scales try the following system:

(a) Memorize the finger pattern.

(b) Slowly repeat the names as you are playing the scale.

(c) Look at the notation as you are slowly playing and saying the names.

(d) Give yourself a random quiz. Be sure to use the same fingers as the scale. This step is extremely important.

(e) Improvise for a while using only scale notes.

Once the warmup scale is mastered, with the correct fingering and the new area of the fingerboard is memorized, play the song or songs that follow. Be sure to finger the notes the same way you did in the scale. Circled numbers represent strings. Uncircled numbers represent fingers. Roman numerals designate positions. (S) means finger stretch. You may use either pick or classical, right hand, technique. If the latter is chosen, use the rest stroke, alternating i & m and/or m & a.

Movable scale forms are used extensively in position studies, especially the following three, one with the root on the ⑥th string and two with the root on the ⑤th string:

Example: Key of G II Position

finger: 2   4   1   2   4   1   3   4   1   3   4   2   4   1   2   4

string: ⑥   ⑤   ④   ③   ②   ①

Example: Key of C II Position

                                                        (s)

finger: 2   4   1   2   4   1   3   4   2   4   1   2   4

string: ⑤   ④   ③   ②   ①

Example: Key of D II Position

finger: 4   1   3   4   1   3   1   2   4   1   2   4

string: ⑤ ④   ③   ②   ①

LEFT HAND FINGERING

Different keys have particular positions that often work best. The following table lists the more common keys on the left and the best positions to play in them on the right:

Key of	*C*	*and relative minor*	*Am*	*=*	*V or VII position*
Key of	*G*	*and relative minor*	*Em*	*=*	*II, VII or IX position*
Key of	*D*	*and relative minor*	*Bm*	*=*	*IV, VII or IX position*
Key of	*A*	*and relative minor*	*F#m*	*=*	*IV or IX position*
Key of	*E*	*and relative minor*	*C#m*	*=*	*IV, VI or IX position*
Key of	*F*	*and relative minor*	*Dm*	*=*	*V or VII position*
Key of	*Bb*	*and relative minor*	*Gm*	*=*	*III or X position*
Key of	*Eb*	*and relative minor*	*Cm*	*=*	*III, V or VIII position*

CHAPTER ONE   BASIC STUDIES

LESSON ONE: II Position

As we mentioned earlier, position is determined by the fret where the first finger naturally falls. In other words, in position I, the first finger goes to the first fret, the second finger goes to the second fret, third finger goes to the third fret, fourth finger goes to the fourth fret. There may be some changes to deal with in certain situations, but this is a general format. In II position that whole format shifts up one fret, i.e. first finger goes to the second fret, second finger goes to the third fret, third finger to fourth fret, fourth finger to fifth fret. As you travel up the fingerboard, ("up" in sound) the frets get closer together. II position studies will be the most difficult physically, because instead of using open strings, we will be reaching with the fourth finger more.

Fill out the fingerboard sheet on the next page. Play, diagram and notate only the natural notes (no sharps or flats). Work with one string at a time up to the sixth fret. Be sure to start with correct open string notation. The first four on the ⑥th string are completed examples. Check yourself with the completed sheet in the back of the book. Pay particularly close attention to the notes on the fifth fret, as this is an important reference or pivot point for mastering the entire fingerboard. Notice also that there is only one natural note on the sixth fret: (F) ②nd string. The open string notes used in I position are also found on the string above (down in sound) fifth fret, except for (B) which is found on the fourth fret. In other words, (E)①string open can also be played on the ② string, fifth fret. The (B) ② string open can also be played on the ③ string, fourth fret. The (G) ③ string open can also be played on the ④ string, fifth fret. (D) ④ string open can also be played on the ⑤ string, fifth fret. (A) ⑤ string open can also be played on the ⑥ string, fifth fret. There is no other place to play (E) ⑥ string open as that is the lowest note on the guitar in normal tuning.

When the fingerboard sheet is completed, proceed to the studies. Memorize the scale with the proper fingering and then practice the tunes. Use the same fingering as the warmup scale.

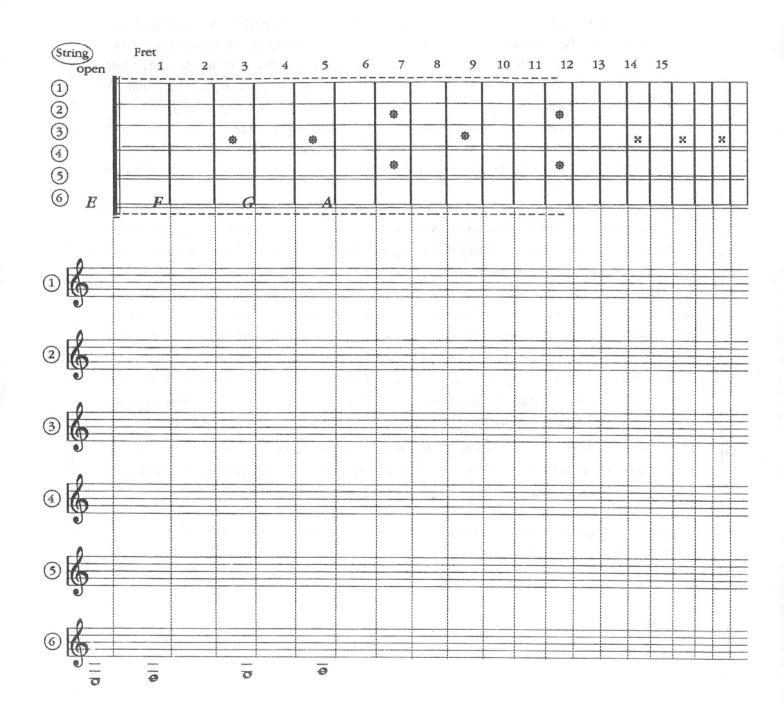

[1] *E MINOR (Em) SCALE II POSITION*

(relative to G major)

finger: 1   3   4   1   3   4   2   4

[2] *"SENECA AUTUMN"*

Be sure to start with
your 1st finger.

R.L.Scicchitano

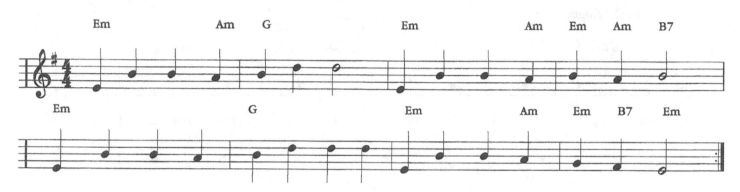

[3] *"HALLOWEEN NIGHT"*

Hold the (B) down in the first line.

Be sure to start with
the 4th finger.

R. L. S.

[4] *D MINOR (Dm) SCALE II POSITION*
(relative to F Major)

Be sure to start on the
⑤ string.

nger: 4   1   2   4   1   2   4   2

[5] *"STRAWBERRY FESTIVAL"*

Be sure to start with
the 2nd finger.

RLS

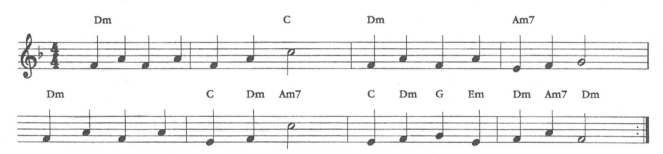

[6] *C MAJOR (C) SCALE II POSITION*

2   4   1   2   4   1   3   4

[7] *"THE LONGHOUSE IN WINTER"*

Be sure to start with
the 2nd finger.

RLS

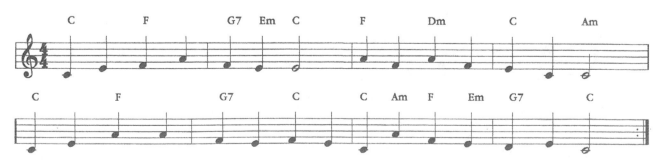

–4–

[8] *A MINOR (Am) SCALE II POSITION*

(relative to C major)

Be sure to start on the
⑥ string.

finger: 4   1   2   4   1   2   4   1

[9] *"ERIE DANCE"*

Be sure to start with
the 4th finger.

RLS

[10] *G MAJOR SCALE II POSITION*

This two octave scale form is one of three
most used in this method. Remember the F#.

2   4   1   2   4   1   3   4   1   3   4   2   4   1   2

Corresponding chord form:

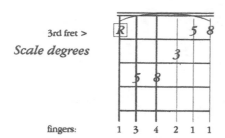

3rd fret >

Scale degrees

fingers: 1 3 4 2 1 1

[11] *"SPRINGTIME IN FEBRUARY"*

Be sure to start with
the second finger.

R.L. Scicchitano

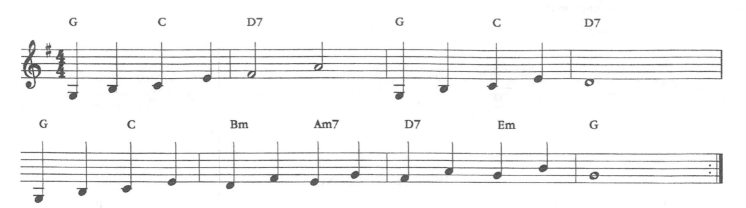

LESSON TWO   III   POSITION.

[1] *C SCALE* (partial)   *III POSITION.*

Be sure to start on the
③ string.

finger: 3   1   3   4   1   3   2

[2] *"GROUND HOG DAY"*   III position

R.L. Scicchitano

[3] *"VALENTINES DAY"*   III position.

Start with the
3rd finger.

RLS

[4] *"THE IIIrd CHRISTMAS"* **III position**

R.L. Scicchitano

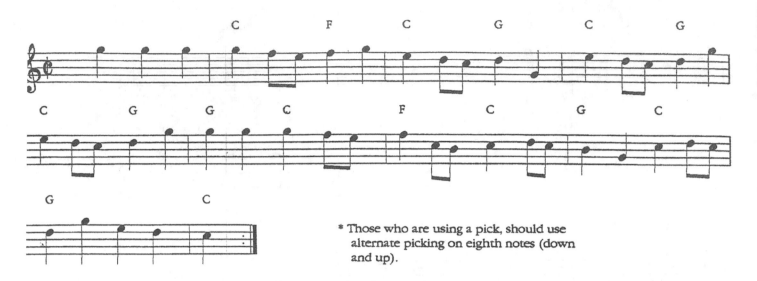

* Those who are using a pick, should use
alternate picking on eighth notes (down
and up).

[5] *"ST. PATRICKS DAY ROCK"* *Dorian mode*

III Position.

Be sure to start with the 3rd finger,
⑤ string.

RLS

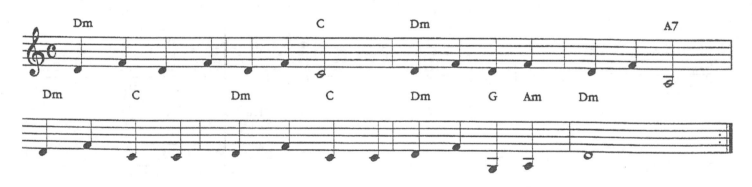

LESSON THREE   *V Position.*

Fill out the fingerboard sheet one string at a time up to the 8th fret. Use the same procedure as the previous sheet. Play, diagram and notate only the natural notes.

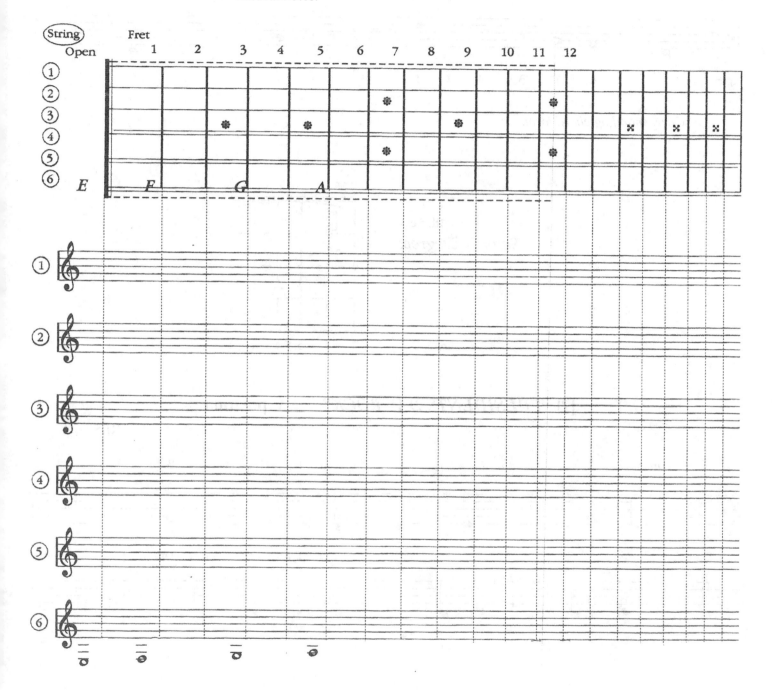

[1] *Dm SCALE V POSITION*

(relative to F major)

Be sure to start on the
⑤ string.

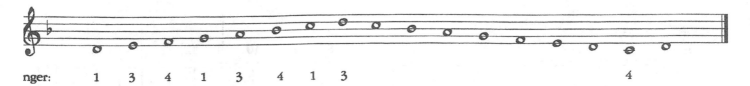

nger: 1   3   4   1   3   4   1   3   4

Corresponding chord form:

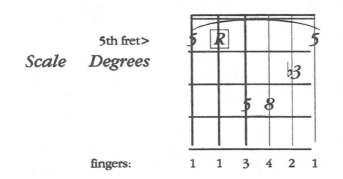

5th fret>
Scale   Degrees

fingers: 1   1   3   4   2   1

[2] *"PRESIDENTS DAY ROCK"*   **V position.**

Dm   B♭

Dm   C   Dm   Em   Dm7   Am7   Dm

4

[3] "EASTER WALTZ"

R.L. Scicchitano

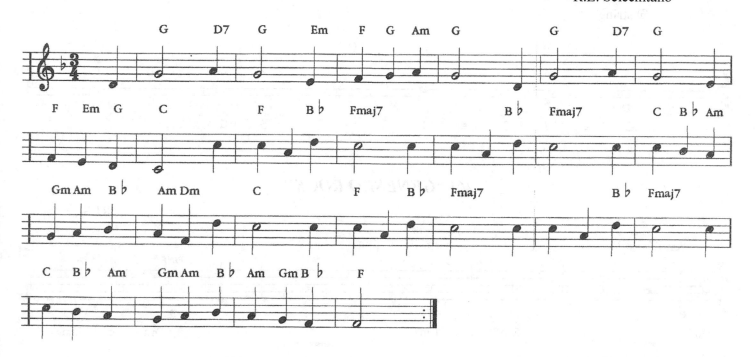

[4] "BATTLESHIP"

RLS

[5] *A MINOR SCALE*   V **position**

Be sure to start on the
⑥ string.

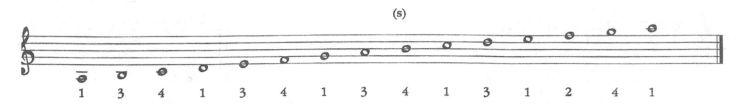

1   3   4   1   3   4   1   3   4   1   3   1   2   4   1

[6] *"GENESEO ROCK"*

RLS

[7] *IMPROVISING*

A most rewarding and challenging area of music is improvising; the art of spontaneous composition. When the scale and melody (notes) to "GENESEO ROCK" are mastered, have someone play the rhythm for you (chords) or record and play back the rhythm. Repeat several times. A good basic rhythm is a steady down strum for each beat. Make up a melody as you go along using only scale notes. Do not be hesitant with simplicity or repetition. Those are good in beginning improvising. Focus and listen closely. As you gain more experience and knowledge, your ears will get sharper. You can anticipate or plan on what you are going to play. You will also, eventually, use more refined tools such as; chord notes, chromatic notes, guide tones (3rd and 7th chord degrees) and melodic embellishment.

[8] *Here is an example of an improvisation*
on "Geneseo Rock"

"THE BIG TREE" is another good tune for improvising. When the melody is mastered
in V position, try this format: Play through the first part as written. Improvise on the repeat
and through the second part. Then go back to the written melody on the D.C.

[9] *"THE BIG TREE"*   **V position**

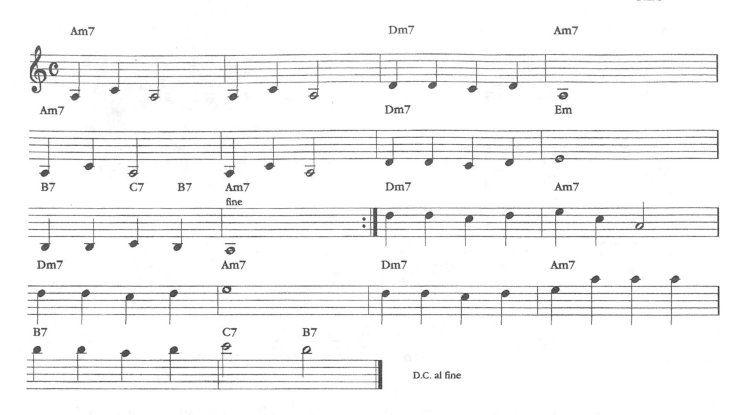

[10] *"NEW YEARS RESOLUTION"*   **Key of C**   **V position**

Be sure to start on the 1st finger,

④ string. Use precise timing.   R.L.Scicchitano

(^) = up pick.

[11] *G DORIAN MODE (minor)*   V position
(related to F major)

Be sure to start on the
④ string.

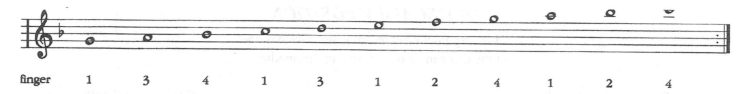

finger   1   3   4   1   3   1   2   4   1   2   4

[12] *"DORIAN HALLOWEEN FUNK"*   V position

Be sure to start with
your 4th finger.

R.L.Scicchitano

CHAPTER TWO   Intermediate Studies.

LESSON ONE

[1] F SCALE V POSITION

This very important movable scale form is one
of the three most used forms in this method.

Be sure to start on the   Don't forget the Bb.
⑤ string.

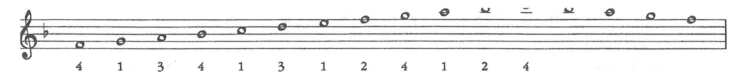

4   1   3   4   1   3   1   2   4   1   2   4

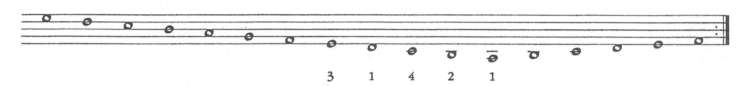

3   1   4   2   1

Corresponding chord form:

5th fret >

Scale degrees

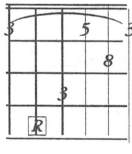

fingers: 1   4   3   1   2   1

[2] *"RAKES OF MALLOW"*

Traditional

[3] *"GREIGSVILLE FLING"*

R.L.Scicchitano

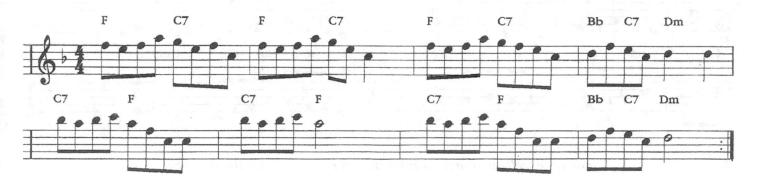

[4] For "LETCHWORTH MAGIC", we will use the natural Dm scale in V position for warm up. Another name for this is the Aeolian mode. It is the same as F major scale except that you will start and end on D; 5 th string, 1ˢᵗ finger.

Corresponding chord form:

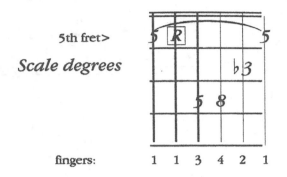

5th fret>

Scale degrees

fingers: 1   1   3   4   2   1

[5] *"LETCHWORTH MAGIC"*

R.L.Scicchitano

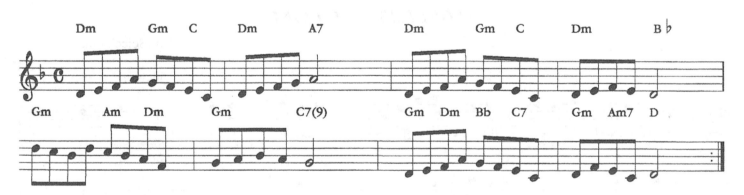

For an excellent source of information on chords see the author's publication:

"ALMOST EVERYTHING ABOUT GUITAR CHORDS."

*   *   *   *   *

LESSON TWO

[1] *Key of D (major) IV position.*

(Don't forget the sharps)

⑤

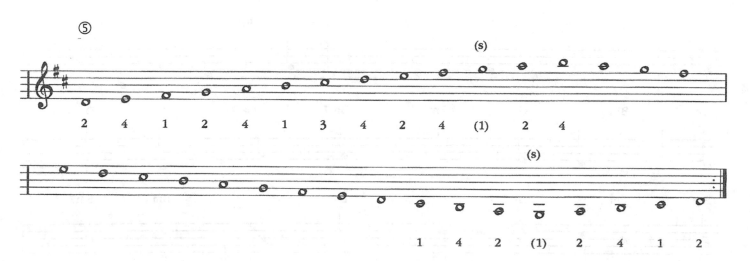

Corresponding chord form:

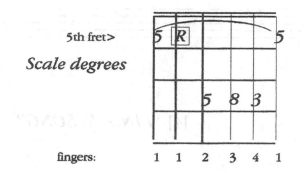

5th fret >

Scale degrees

fingers:

[2] *"D MAJOR IN THE 50's"*

R.L.Scicchitano

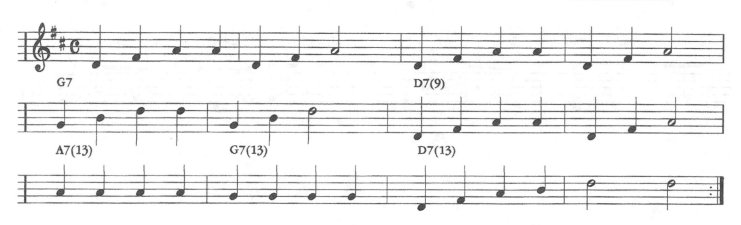

[3] *"HEMLOCK MORNING"* IV Position

(Don't forget the f# and c#)

Be sure to start with the 1st finger
④ string, fourth fret.

R.L.Scicchitano

[4] *"LINDA'S SONG"* IV Position.

RLS

LESSON THREE   V POSITION REVIEW

F major scale warm up

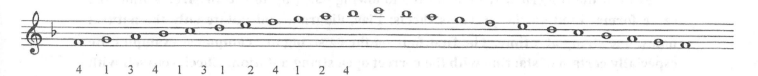

[1] "CARDUELIS TRISTIS"

R.L. Scicchitano

LESSON FOUR   *VII POSITION*

   This is probably the most important position, due to its strategic location on the fingerboard and the proximity of the frets.

   Fill out the fingerboard sheet on the following page, up to the 10th fret. Follow the same format used on the previous sheets: Play, diagram and notate only the natural notes, one string at a time. The first four on the ⑥ string are completed examples. Be especially certain of starting with the correct open string notation. Check yourself with the completed sheet in the back of the book.

[1] G SCALE VII POSITION

(This is the same scale form that is often used
for the key of F, V position.)

Don't forget the F#

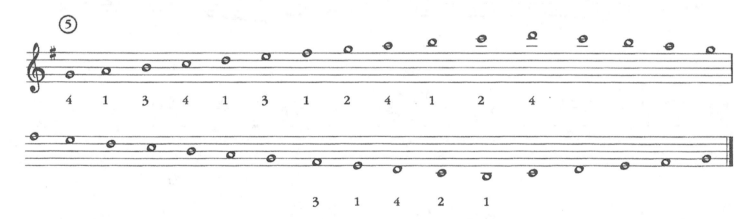

Corresponding chord form:

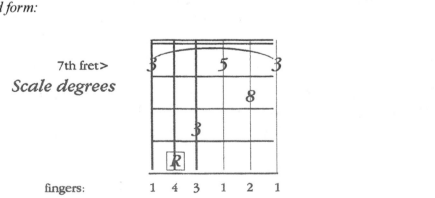

7th fret>
Scale degrees

fingers: 1 4 3   1 2 1

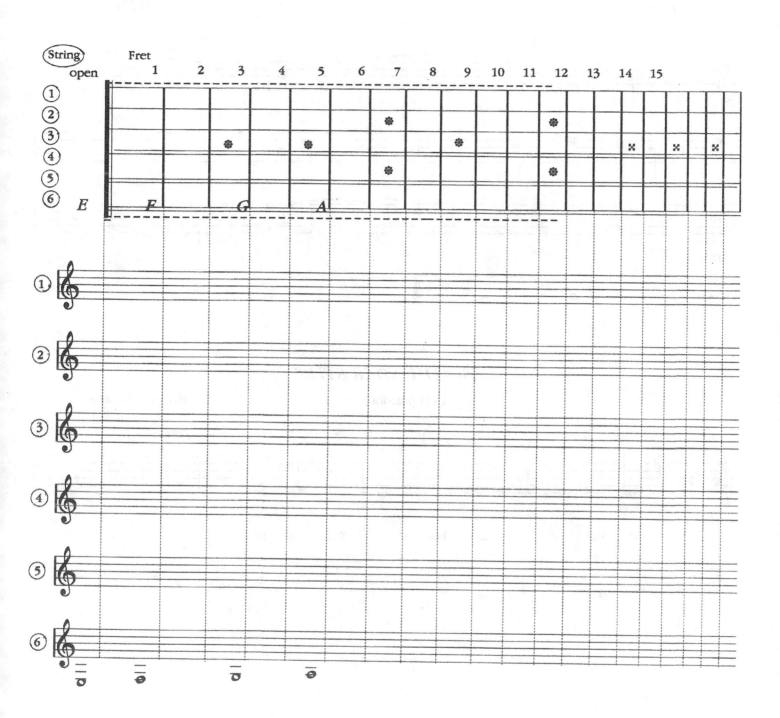

[2] *"WHEN THE SAINTS GO MARCHING IN"*
(VII Position)

⑤   Traditional

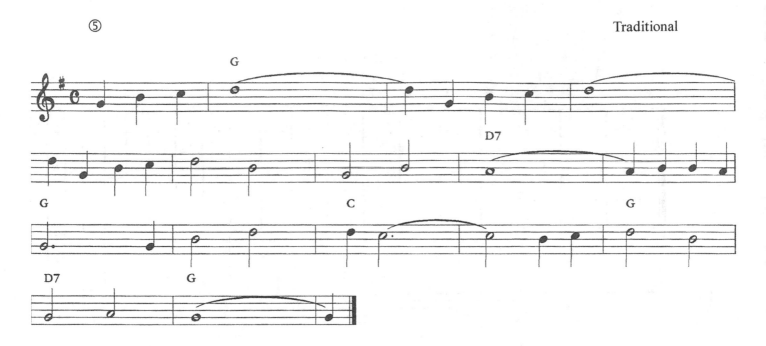

[3] *"THUNDER RITE"*
(VII position)

R.L.Scicchitano

[4] *"ROCK ISLAND REEL"**   **VII Position**

Be sure to start on the 3rd finger,   Traditional
④ string.

> *   A reel is a dance common in North America and Northern Europe
> usually in a medium fast duple meter.

[5] *"ALPINE MEADOWS"*   **VII position**

Be sure to start on the 3rd finger   R.L.Scicchitano
④ string.

[6] *"EMIGRANT'S REEL"*   VII position

Traditional

[7] *"OLD CROW"*   VII position

Be sure to start on the 1st finger
③ string.

Traditional Irish reel

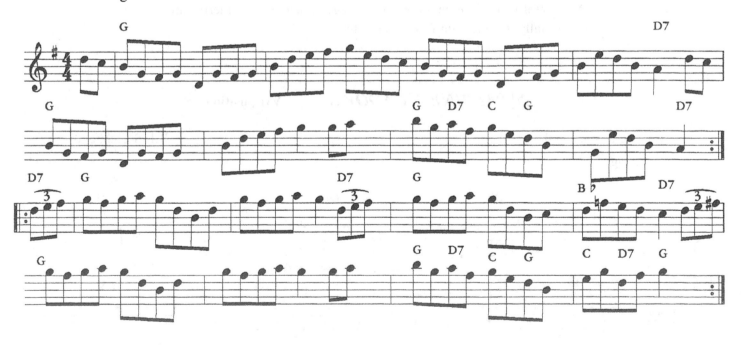

[8] *E MINOR SCALE (natural)*   VII POSITION

(relative to G major)

Don't forget F#.

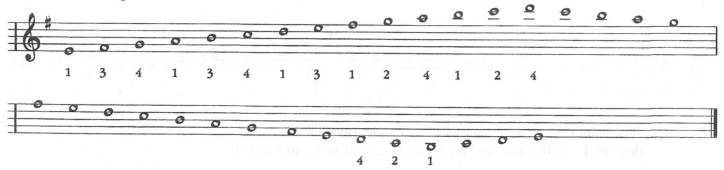

Corresponding chord form:

7th fret>
Scale degrees

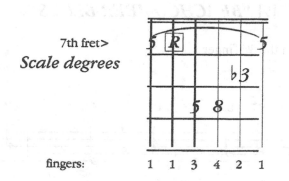

fingers: 1 1 3 4 2 1

[9] *"WINTER SONG"*   VII position

R.L.Scicchitano

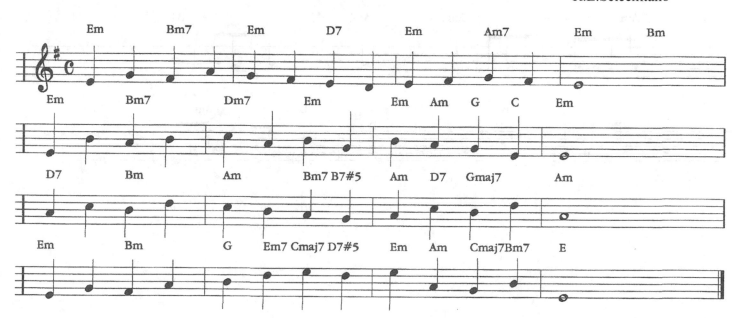

[8] *E BLUES SCALE*   VII POSITION
(G pentatonic)*

Blue Notes

b3   b7

1   4   1   3   1   3   2   4   1   4   4   1

* A pentatonic scale is the same as a major scale without the 4th and 7th
  degrees. It has five notes and is used in music with little chord activity.

[9] *"BEACHCOMBER BLUES"*   VII position

Be sure to start on the 3rd finger   R.L.Scicchitano
④ string.

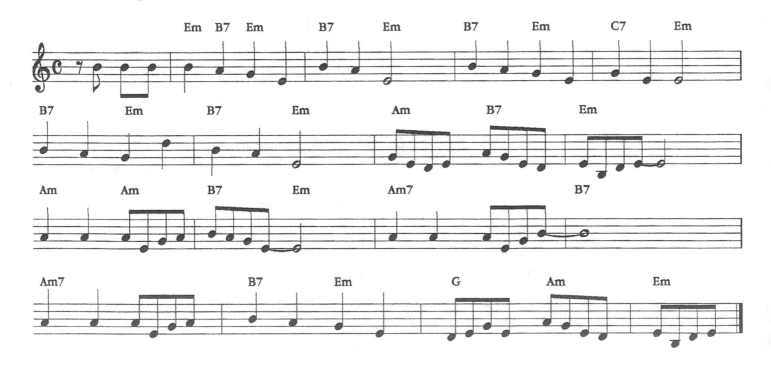

LESSON FIVE

[1] *A MAJOR (A) SCALE*   IV POSITION

Don't forget the F#,C#,and G#.

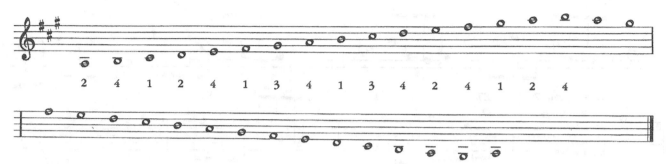

Corresponding chord form:

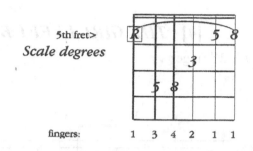

5th fret>
Scale degrees

fingers: 1   3   4   2   1   1

---

* Another important way of mastering scale forms is to practice playing through the scale starting and ending on different degrees. This will give you a more thorough perspective of the scale form, and will also teach you the modes: Starting and ending on the 2nd degree will give you the Dorian mode; the 3rd degree will give you the Phrygian; starting and ending on the 4th degree will produce the Lydian mode; the 5th degree will be the Mixolydian mode; the 6th will be the Aeolian mode and the 7th will be the Locrian mode.

---

[2] *"WALKING THE BULLDOG"*   IV position

R.L.Scicchitano

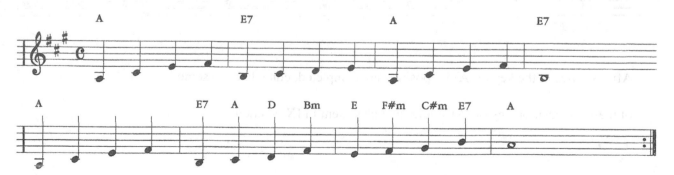

[3] *"SLEIGH RIDE"* IV position

Be sure to start on the 4th finger
④ string, 7th fret.

R.L.Scicchitano

[4] *"THE GIRL I LEFT BEHIND"*

Be sure to start on the 2nd finger
① string, 5th fret.

Traditional

After studies in the key of (A) IX position are completed, come back to some

of these IV position key of (A) studies and play them in IX position.

[5] *"LAMPLIGHTER HORNPIPE"**   IV position

Traditional

* A Hornpipe is a dance performed with folded arms and many characteristic steps and gestures. It was popular in England from the 16th through 19th centuries.

Often Jigs, Reels and Hornpipes are written in sixteen notes and duple meter to give a fasterfester impression. Here is "LAMPLIGHTER HORNPIPE" written in notation more typical of this style.

LESSON SIX

[1] C SCALE   VII POSITION

Be sure to start on the 2nd finger, 8th fret,
⑥ string.

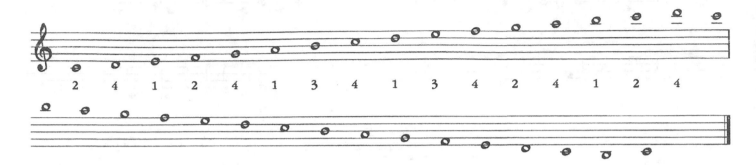

Corresponding chord form:

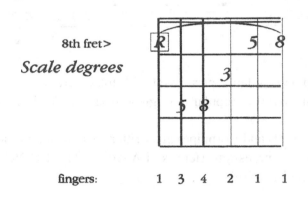

8th fret>

Scale degrees

fingers: 1   3   4   2   1   1

[2] "EVENING BIRDS"   VII position

Be sure to start on the 2nd finger, 8th fret,
① string.

R.L.Scicchitano

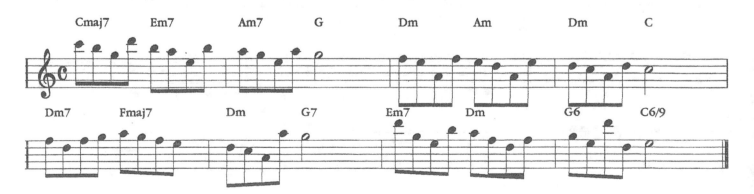

[3] *"PERPETUAL CLIMBING"*   VII position

R.L.Scicchitano

[4] *"SALAMANCA REEL"*   VII position

Be sure to start on 4th finger, 10th fret,   Traditional
④ string.

[5] *"NEW ORLEANS HOLIDAY"*   **VII position**

Be sure to start on the 4th finger, 10th fret, ④ string.

R.L.Scicchitano

[6] *"COME HASTE TO THE WEDDING"*   **VII position**

Be sure to start on the 4th finger, 10th fret ⑤ string.

Traditional jig

[7] *"CHINA HOUSE"*   **VII position**

Be sure to start on the 4th finger, 10th fret,
④ string.

R.L.Scicchitano

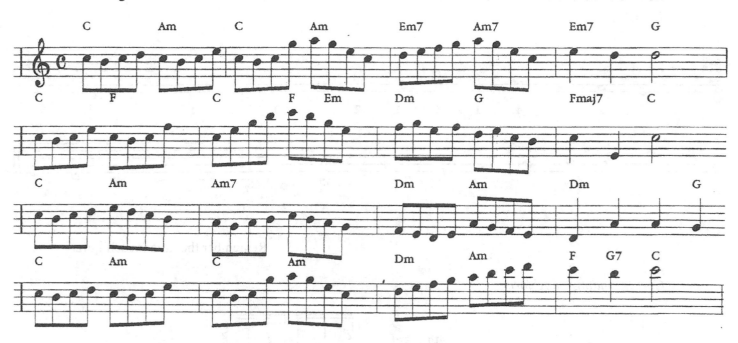

[8] *"PADDY CAREY"*

Be sure to start on the 4th finger, 10th fret,
⑤ string.

Tradition Irish jig

LESSON SEVEN
[1] E MAJOR SCALE   IV POSITION

Be sure to start on the 7th fret,
⑤ string.

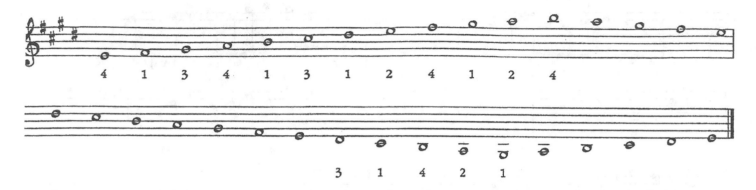

4   1   3   4   1   3   1   2   4   1   2   4

3   1   4   2   1

Remember the random self quiz.

Corresponding chord form:

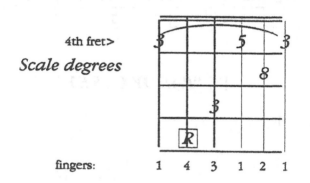

4th fret>

Scale degrees

fingers: 1   4   3   1   2   1

[2] *"GOLDEN SLIPPERS"*   IV position

Be sure to start on the 2nd finger, 5th fret,
② string

Traditional
Reharmonization by RLS

[3] *"BIRDS IN FLIGHT"*   IV position

R.L.Scicchitano

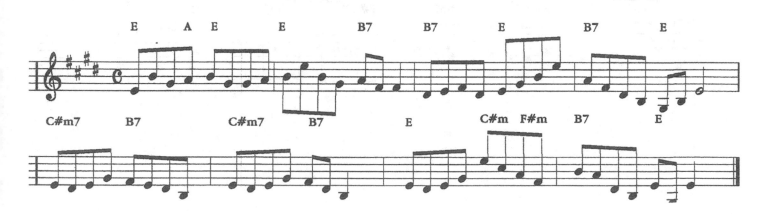

[4] *"IRISH WASHERWOMAN"*   **IV position**

Be sure to start on the 1st finger.   Traditional jig

[5] *"CHORD CLIMBING WITH AN UNEXPECTED LANDING"*

R.L.Scicchitano

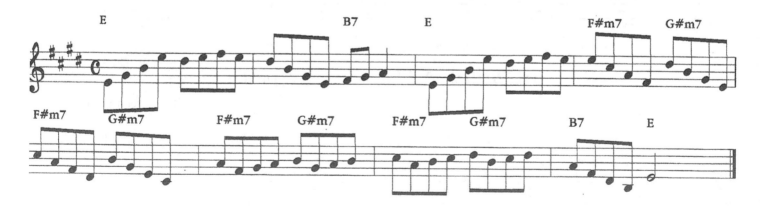

LESSON EIGHT
[1] *Bb MAJOR SCALE*   *V POSITION*

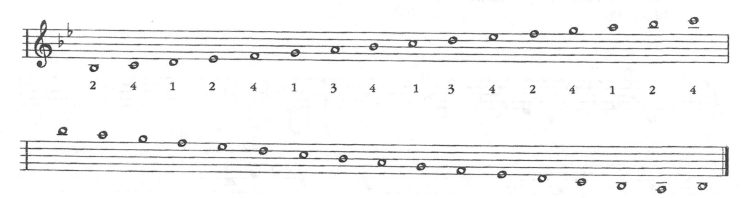

Corresponding chord form:

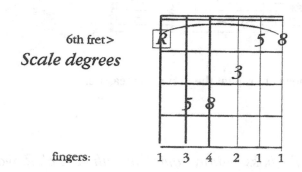

6th fret>

Scale degrees

fingers: 1   3   4   2   1   1

[2] *"ZACH's TUNE"*   V position.

Be sure to start on the 4th finger, 8th fret,
④ string.

RLS

[3] *"BASS ROCK"*   V position.

Don't forget that the key of Bb has
Bb and Eb.

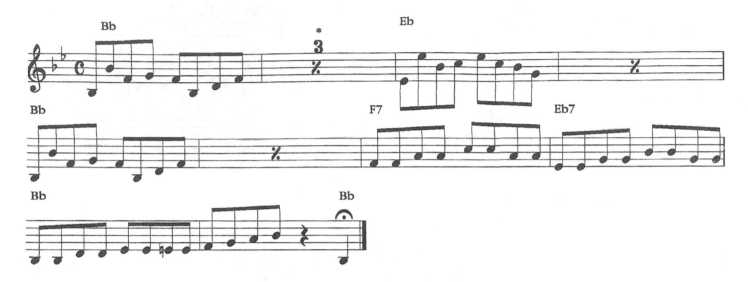

* This means to repeat the previous measure.

Transposition for bass guitar, complete with bass cleff, would look like this:

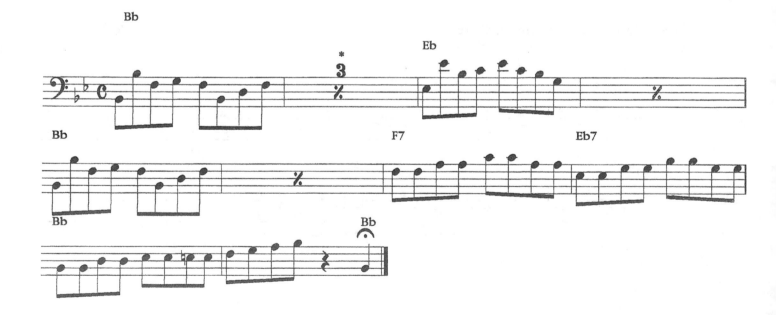

[4] *"NEW CENTURY HORNPIPE"*   **V position**

Be sure to start on the 4th finger, 8th fret,
⑤ string.

Traditional

[5] *"SUE's SONG"*   **V position**

R.L.Scicchitano

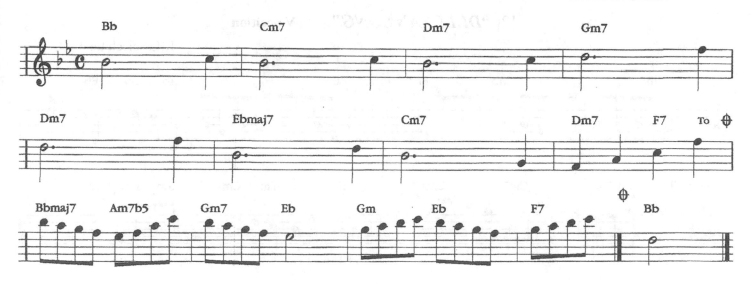

LESSON NINE

[1] *Eb MAJOR SCALE*   *V POSITION*

This key has three flats; Bb, Eb, and Ab.

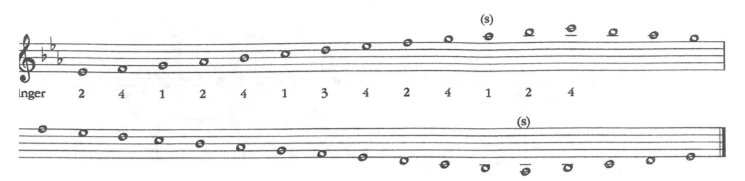

inger   2   4   1   2   4   1   3   4   2   4   1   2   4

Corresponding chord form:

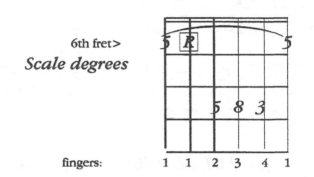

6th fret>
Scale degrees

fingers:

[2] *"DELENA's SONG"*   **V position**

R.L.Scicchitano

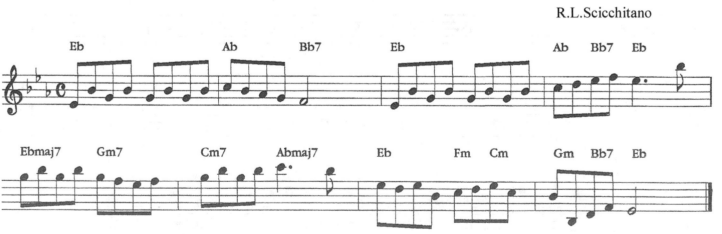

[3] *"THE SHERWOOD POLKA"*   V position or VI

Be sure to start on the 2nd finger, 6th fret,   R.L.Scicchitano
⑤ string.

For III position review, practice "The Sherwood Polka" in that position
as well as V position.

[4] *"THE LIVINGSTON WALTZ"*   V position

RLS

* Be sure to stretch the first finger back to the fourth fret.

At this time, go back and review the VII position lessons. Then you will be
ready to go on to IX position.

LESSON TEN   *IX Position.*

Fill out the fingerboard sheet one string at a time, up to the 12ᵗʰ fret. Play, diagram and notate only the natural notes.

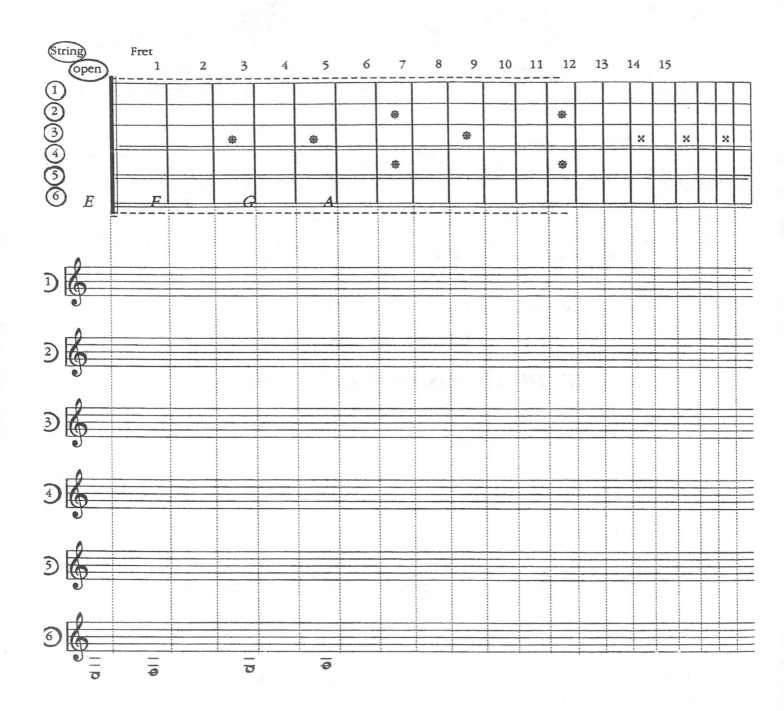

[1] *A MAJOR SCALE IX POSITION*
(F# C# G#)

Be sure to start on the 4th finger, 12th fret,
⑤ string.

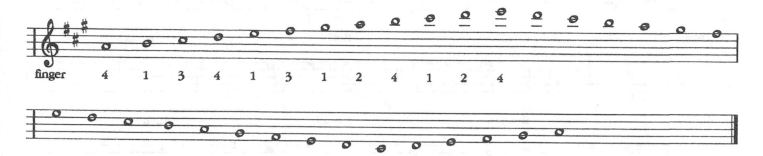

Don't forget the random self quiz.

Corresponding chord form:

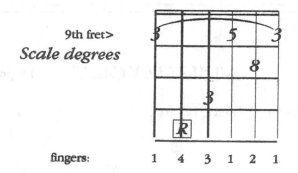

9th fret>
Scale degrees

fingers: 1   4   3   1   2   1

[2] *"THE OLD MADRID"*   IX position.

R.L.Scicchitano

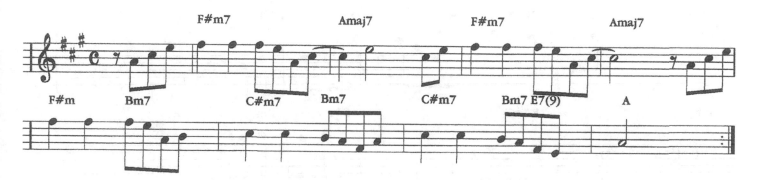

[3] *"ALLEGENY MORNING"*   IX position

R.L.Scicchitano

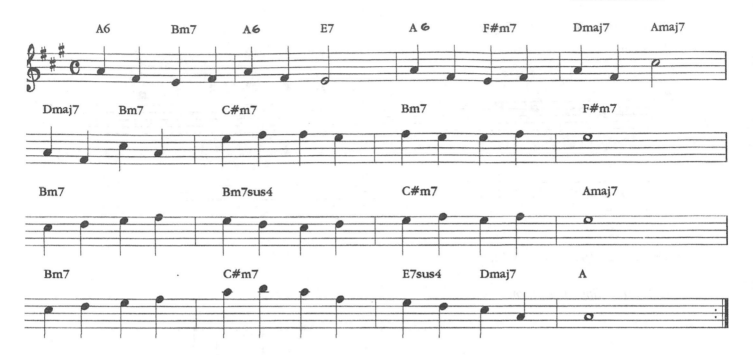

[4] *"VALLEY CALL"*   IX position

Be sure to start on the 4th finger, 12th fret,
① string.

RLS

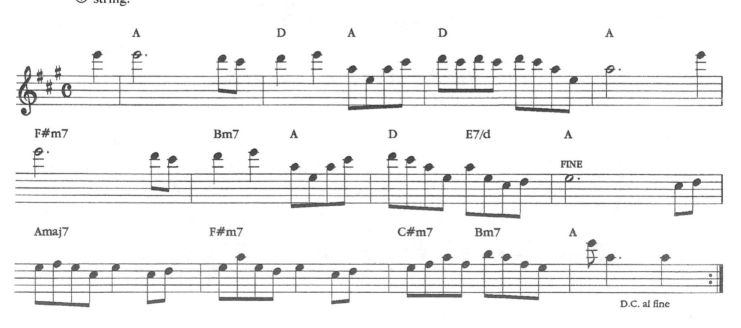

[5] *"THE GENESEE VALLEY POLKA"*   **IX position**

Be sure to start on the 3rd finger, 11th fret,   RLS
④ string.

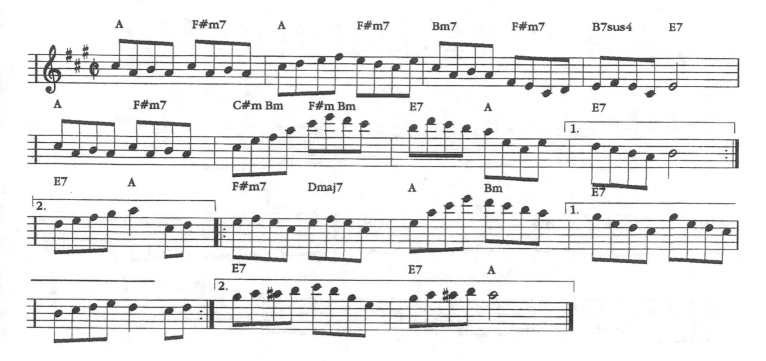

[6] *"DICK SAND's HORNPIPE"*   **IX position**

Be sure to start on the 1st finger, 9th fret,   Traditional
③ string.

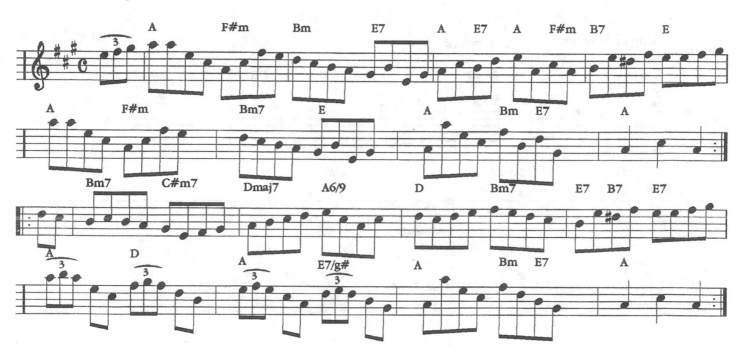

[7] *"DOUG BASSETT's REEL"*   **IX position**

R.L.Scicchitano

* To sound this F#, slide the 4th finger up to the 14th fret.

[8] *"BUZZO's SWING"*   **IX position**

Swing eight notes: RLS

LESSON ELEVEN   *COMBINING POSITIONS*
Pay close attention to position
changes and fingering.

[1] *"A CONESUS JULY 4ᵗʰ"*

Don't forget to check the
key signature.

R.L.Scicchitano

[2] *"HOCHSTEIN BREAK"*

RLS

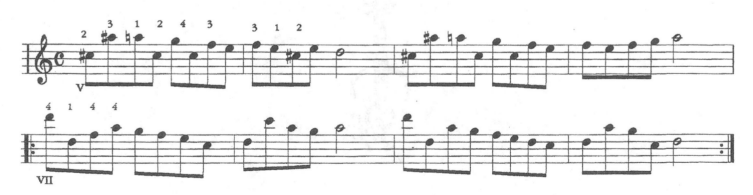

[3] "THE EVERGLADES AT NIGHT"

Pay close attention to positions
and fingering.

RLS

x   This is a double sharp.

*   The rule for accidentals is that they are cancelled
    in the next measure unless they are in the key
    signature.

[4] *"FEUD IN A MAJOR"*

From the Recording album Ralph Louis, Anytime, Anywhere

R.L.Scicchitano

Country Feel

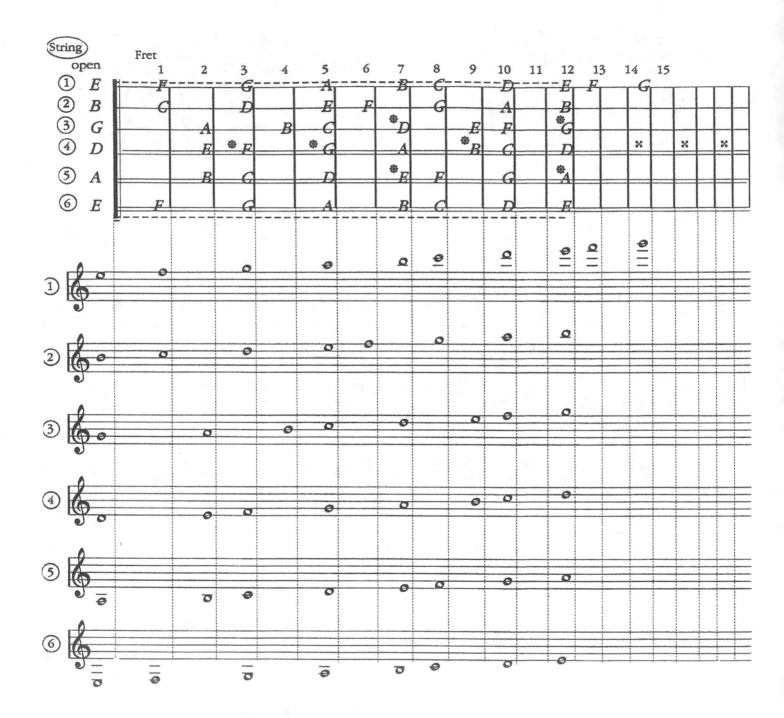

Printed in the United States
By Bookmasters